Without Compass

WITHOUT COMPASS

Benjamin Miller

Four Way Books
Tribeca

Please direct all inquiries to:
Editorial Office
Four Way Books
POB 535, Village Station
New York, NY 10014
www.fourwaybooks.com

Library of Congress Cataloging-in-Publication Data

Miller, Benjamin (Poet)
[Poems. Selections]
Without compass / Benjamin Miller.
pages cm
Includes bibliographical references.
ISBN 978-1-935536-38-3 (alk. paper)
I. Title.
PS3613.I53248A6 2014
811'.6--dc23

2013036089

This book is manufactured in the United States of America and printed on acid-free paper.

Four Way Books is a not-for-profit literary press. We are grateful for the assistance
we receive from individual donors, public arts agencies, and private foundations.

This publication is made possible with funds from the Jerome Foundation.

[clmp]

We are a proud member
of the Council of Literary Magazines and Presses.

Distributed by University Press of New England
One Court Street, Lebanon, NH 03766

Contents

For Sara
who let me finish the hat

I

Desert

What have I been doing? Nothing, nothing.
Look: the blue couch scraped the floorboards
Where we pushed it flush. The empty wall.
The parquet's little screaming.

In a dream all afternoon I dredged the ocean,
Pulling razor clams and wedding rings.
One-eyed crabs clung to my fingers,
And I named them. This is wait. This, delay.

I found the perfect flaw and brought it home.
Like falling kites, the night came in a rush.

Field Glass (Disassembled)

And you, with all your maps and papers,
thinking me afraid.

Go out? Go out? There is no out.
Outside this tent the desert,
and outside the desert, sand.

Desert

Like falling kites, the night came in a rush
To settle just outside the window, garnet eyes
Outlined by swaying trees. Pewter-slow,
My throat contracted. Hidden wings unfurled.

Beneath the pinning sheet we shivered, knew
The door-latch was elusive, almost cruelly
Insubstantial. Soon the curtained glass turned
Delicate; the clock's hand, catlike,

Stretched and flicked a paper tongue.
Before morning came, a tapping.

Persistence as an Accident

The absence of news.
Pavement, and the heat of it
Against your cheek: light

In skin-tight circles.
How we danced, like rain
Or bees describing rain;

Returning, we are always
Here, bound, spun, struck,
Startled by the fleetness of

Desire and its counterfeits,
Bested and diffused.
I do not mean to hate you.

In a less mortal world,
Tree would be equal to
Wind, rocking gently

And *rustle of leaves*
Would never be translated
Crow in its descent.

But here beneath this moon—
Heroically young, pale, stone—
You lie, and won't stop lying.

In the White Noise of the Evening

after Louise Glück

Forget me if I say I'll leave you: the bashful
and never-spoken-to-again are always
riven by static. I cannot prove
what I can't believe, while you discourse of
virtue as if it meant something: you haunt me like the open sea,
never a sane thing in a sane face.
Oh, you were ever lady finger, consonant, laying down
a pale second in the morning beside the nightstand,
and the day before, commanding in the tea box. You couldn't see
us as less used to it, this chatter that inhibits risk
of becoming anything, the Price Club and the Money Tree,
the salt-free chip and thin gravy—were you right to deny
that I could resist? This is
how I cruel you to thought, with this refrain
in the white noise of the evening,
in the creaking ever rocking your chair, the latch
now lifting at the gate.

Field Glass (Manifest)

Westward they'd say
Send your people westward

So we heaped linens packed
Our choices into pinewood boxes
        And left

+

Not knowing whether chills were the reason
We moved so slowly

        Such terrible wonders

Prying dead thumbs with thumbs near-dead themselves

        I'm sorry
        I'm sorry I say such unnecessary things

+

Coming home is not return but arrival
You say but I say home is neither   Home
        is traveling together

+

Still
Wishing evening didn't make me slow
Wishing every night for cheer

She turns toward the window sometimes
And

+

Westward
The horizon remains the same

Were we always this distant

+

Some days I wake
And find you haven't followed

Worse are the days I set out after you

Zoetrope with Unopened Window

Already, table lamps have gone to dust; a ficus
by the window drops its leaves. In the evening

he'll explain the way the power comes and goes,
the way electric light presents but meek resistance

to the wall (the sudden nature of the wall)—
this kind of talk upsets her, when she listens.

Conversation turns to days and years
keep piling up. Their life is a fence

speed has all but made transparent,
the empty space revealed beyond: a flip-book life

he does not dare to show her.

from **Reasons I No Longer Date**

1.

You have no idea
how quickly you can make a fool
of a monkey.

Let me tell you.
It takes longer than you'd think.

5.

My Friday friends don't know me any more
than my school-or-work-related friends
know calculus. Which is to say, they know
a little bit, and more would come back to them
if we ever spoke about it.

8.

Tell you what—let's go down to the cemetery,
no, let's go down to the planetarium, no, let's
second-guess our second-guesses. It's a game
I tend to win.

Lions Will Take You and I Will Not Care

I will lay out all your past misdeeds
and catalogue them: 1. Your legs
do not exist 2. Your tolerance
for luminance is far too limited
by your relationships with women
3. I am not amused. Small animals
have fallen before you in disgust
with less aplomb than you display
before me now, and I the master

here. Brimful of finial, your chair
turns under your weight 4. I saw
your scarf chasing across grounds
itself. This was your fault; the sky
blue cloak you'd offered, clouded,
could not protect me from the sun
reflected off your morning coat.
Did I say nimbus? I meant safe
haven, keyhole for a missing key.

You make the drawing, yes, but
who provides the pen must answer
to it 6. I speak, and you write
nothing. Are you unlettered by my
conversation? Let me not distract
as violins do not distract. Empty
your glass the other half 5. Thought
I'd leave out number five? How easy
it has always been to trick you.

Terminal

No point in waiting for a flight: the planes
have lost their mates, are inconsolable. All
pretense that the shaking sobs were turbulence

has dropped, now they tremble even on the ground.
Just before the turbines, said my neighbor, *air
is coldest.* Through the concourse window

we can see the luggage carts learn new ways
to retrace each other's steps. I've never heard
so many blinking lights before. My cushion

sinks, a wheel into tarmac, but it's better
to slide than to focus on People or Time
or the Self on the lap of a girl to my right.

Morning depresses like a signet into wax.
Breakfast depresses like a doctor on the tongue.
If they could bottle this emotion, I would buy it.

Desert

Before, morning came tapping,
A sharp, repeated pain like a woodpecker.
Now this: dull in-wrapping of the brain,
Blanket dragged across the carpeted halls

Of sleep, and waking to a ragged-ribbon
Sky. If only there were more than night
To talk to, or a third to walk beside us—
But here is only veil and doubt,

And the sound of water, spilling,
In the hollows, futility.

Jacob and the Angels

Again the sudden slick of fear
across the shoulder blades, the ozone scrape
of tooth on tooth, of knowledge on fast wings.
I have never been alone.

I can still see the crowded womb, my brother
thrust forward as a shield against forgetting.
His only birthright was the touch above his lip
instead of mine: coming behind, my eyes

remained open. Believe me: there are worlds
we do not speak about, camps and ladders
everywhere. (The air is overrun.)

What have I done I would not take back.

The Way You Find Me

Understand, it is not with me as it is with bridges.
On mountains haloed by glass at the summit,
I worried the twilight with fletch and quiver;

I missed the dire in misdirection. Now we wake
away from morning, but the morning
pursues. You can't deny you worry, too,

for we are granted absolution
only if we learn to grasp unfolding, and who
can search for what is obvious?

Despite the forces in its favor, we don't admire the moon
for its verisimilitude. We admire its coldness.
The way it smiles and never has to breathe.

Cohortative with Pity

In the voice of the light, the echolalia
Of the windmills of your own mind,
  There's room for what's to come.

To be apprehended is something
  To strive for: you get your terriculaments,

  And you seize them, and you run.
I couldn't sleep at night with them
If they were mine—but then again,

  You must know more than I do about
The world of the ten thousand things.

It wasn't the fuss I wanted. As one
  Well-familiar with the ampersands of night,
It didn't occur to me I could be wrong.

Interview

What do you remember?
I remember edges, receding.

What are edges?
Sunrise over glacial ice.

What is the sun?
A single star does not define an evening.

What is the sun?
I will forsake you, and still you will return to me.

Field Glass (Communion)

He sat with the bayonet for hours,
clenching and unclenching it in the fist
of his chest. His breath showed hot

and chill, trembling on the blade.
He thinks: the sun will never teach
horizons how it climbs, how many

plume moths make a century, how we
disappear. The leaves will burn and fall.
Behind him, bruising light condenses—

he remembers pliant tides, the deep-
sea call of half-familiar faces. Hands
release in offering. Clang of letting go.

Beneath a Shawl of Gathered Wool

Look at me: in debt to a god
for an unguided tour of doorways,
decks, and curtains, this god who withholds

nothing from the empty-hearted
rats that rive and nestle in the leaves.
He sends me gifts that torment

all the neighbors, who—I mean no harm—
have all gone somewhat mad. This morning
I received a scantish crowd of buffalo

but revived no faster for the audience.
Outside, the grass was trampled
into shallow bowls: an offering?

I drink in a silence like the felling of trees
unnoticed. This is not a house of prayer,
nor has it been, but how the penitent

refuse to hear it! Fridays they present
their hapless plea: *Let there be tables,*
and a broken hole where we will seat you,

kiss you with our purpose; let us
shelter you among the ragweed billow,
smooth away your locks and bars.

It is not within my nature to deny
the hopeless entry. So I confess,
it is a terrible blow to be present,

if unlikely to happen again, for
this isn't wholly life, these careful plots
that earn me but a simple, well, a weakness.

Wake *up*: you're being lectured to.
Now we're forgetting our fables all over again,
how every minute of quiet means the death

of a cardinal, the sermons
of glass-dead birds. Habit keeps
my name from the public.

Habit the sting on the bee.

Desert

In the hollows, futility—
See the stones you gathered
Fall to one side of the hill,
And then another. See wolves

Pursue the sun's redundant toss;
They won't return. Because
Corrupt and clouded auguries
Have never failed to please you,

Had you been allotted strength,
Not even I would know the truth.

Desert

Now, even I don't know the truth,
But if illusions offer comfort it is this:
I do not need it. Intimations of the thaw
Abound—the shards and misreflections

Of another age that fade into cuneiform
Cracks on the bathroom door. The blue
Couch with its rings beneath the cushions—
From the rain. You know you are entitled

To this wounded sense of drowsiness,
And I? I am a fool: a disbeliever.

Numerology

ONE On an outing to New England, any reason is enough.

TWO High-tension wires overhead swaying to birdsong.

THREE Rewinding the film yet again. Threat of the reel not catching.

FOUR Of all the hours we shared, why assign this one to me?

FIVE If ever I have feared, I have lived through it. I will

SIX Live through this. Threat of stitches catching.

SEVEN Eventually, night will overtake the van. Will you never see?

EIGHT Against the pane, a draught caught, a clutch.

NINE This is not real. This is not real. This is not

TEN Night, ripping the van open like a net—

Interview

What have you forgotten?
I have lost confidence. It is a foreign art.

What is lost confidence?
The paper folded on a thousand lines.

What is a thousand?
In your palm, each grain of sand is like a face.

What is a face?
I watch her turn into the light.

In the Place of Best Intentions

As this is not the land of ice packs
and regenerations, of spent glue guns

or antiseptic counters—since shy
reminders filter through the streets all night

(mountain streams that city fountains sip)
absconding with old disappointments—

because the powerlines are wet with flames
that spill their music into shallow halls

devoid of short-term motives, I am lost
and cannot say what may have led me here

to watch the girls unwrapping fiberboard
from miles of burlap while the waitresses

tattoo their angry daisies on my arms.
What is this place that leaves me so unmoved?

A hat I'd never worn or wanted worn
is now my prized possession; tissues packed

into abandoned zipper pockets breed—
I had forgotten that the small glass cups

were hidden in my socks and that my hands
were laced with fine red scratches

long before the advent of arrival. Now I feel
the heat of my illusion dim to tremble,

a dull intrusion into some romantic
basement of unknowable books. And so

forgive me if the water left for tea
is steeped in silt and valentines; forgive

the unexpected token undisclosed.
Last night I thought I wanted tragedy,

a chance to wick away the morning's
donut, bagel, muffin, scorn. But to span

the gap from night to night, from night
to some hello, is more than I can yet

achieve: a phone that rings without response
and without end or empathy.

Belief is a raft tossed out on a thirsty plain.
Were I that lonesome, I'd never have left.

It Rained Tonight

and so I thought of you

somewhere under a streetlamp,
your attention elsewhere—

upward, toward the ticker tape
of rain, halted

as by flashbulbs, lightning
in your eyes, your hair, your

hands holding the umbrella
upside down, forgotten,

so it falls, too heavy with the water.

Self-Portrait as Forewarned Caesar

For all that you have been ambitious, was there ever a need?
The orange lights were not searching for you,
Nor were they there to call you home.
Collect your thoughts: the final hour clears its throat
And starts the long approach.

IV

Dinner in the Uncanny Valley

The waiter mouths apologies and smiles across the room.
A pretty girl? A colleague? When you turn,
your elbow brushes plastic, yielding just a moment late
into a tablecloth. The expected waitress isn't there.
In her hair your date has set a peacock feather like an owl's
eye, a hawk's. Over clinking forks and glasses
conversation hums and ticks impeccably.
Look up, you tell yourself, *the waiter will be waiting.*

Misconception

I had never seen a trampoline. The walls
were made of ladders and the floor
was filled with sand. A violinist playing

on the beach (the second movement of
The Planets, or the last) inspired a bonfire
which the brass provided.

Starfish, divided, multiplied, thrilled
by the vibrato. Curling toes against the tide,
everyone clapping stopped.

In a Recurring Dream of Winged Ascent

Sirens and flares reflect
    blue-white off windows
opposite. How sense is dulled

by repetition, hammers
    in the pulse that etch out
your epitaph: a single word

ad infinitum. Across the wall
    blackbird-shadows panic,
always from right to left,

always the same unfolding
    suicide of origami light.
May this, then, be your gift:

to notice, when the images have gone,
    that they were on their way—
and knew where they were going.

Persistence as an Acolyte

1. Sketches

Travels slowly and fasts often. Suffers from early hair loss and a sense of easy satisfaction. In the morning, prone to dreams of falling; the feeling of imbalance holds the day long.

Owns simple clothes: only suit is brown, and for a necktie must ask friends. Knows many songs. All sound the same except when someone else is singing them.

Optimist.

Embarrassment.

2. Mission

Was approached some years ago while in the marketplace, a vigorous city of small tents and walls adorned with wooden hedgehogs, rugs, and candles, by a seller of books and crimson robes. The robe, he thought, would look nice on my shelf, but—

The salesman read aloud a pilgrimage, naming stops: Firepit. Brambles. Grainpath. Lake. In the end the robe was not, in fact, but made a decent blanket for the journey, there and back.

3. Scenes and Situations

> At the Local Inn
> London Birdbath: His Reflection There
> In the Courtyard of the Monastery
> Mountainous
> Heather, Hyacinth, Rosemary, Rose
> Final Night of Summer Constellations
> Echo

4. Childhood and Adolescence

were the same.

5. During Which He Makes a Resolution

Ahead, the climbing road; the camp behind
    the hedgerow was behind.
In a way, it made him glad to have
    as traveling companion no one
else: it gave him time to think:

6. On the Path

The grain was not grain. It was grass,
brown-stemmed and taller than a child.
Here and there within the timothy a thistle,
with a mantis on a leaf. From these
he learned humility. And bristle.

On the Margins of the Portable Country

The making of ideology, of how stories learn,
ends in bone. Thus, facts without lives are trouble.
Even squall, the art of, must learn to scramble hours

as the scribblers do; and so some argument electric
in its innocence arrives to silver fictions
out of mauve and maudlin discipline.

All worthy hearts embark. But who returns
from such a journey—who could tent beneath
that zoo and cairn with time's fool law

and still press on unscathed? (The lathe, the nick,
the cutting tree remembering the cutting.)
On the margins of the portable country,

a stranger compendium lands its craft
of pleasure and scorn, a balloon
in love with a wood, a turtle fallen

from the subjunctive into the academy.
I've started marking up a manual of dangers.
You have not all been selected.

Intimations of the Thaw

1.

The plow grieves. A fish leaps over a hook.
A scattering.
Before we set sail a man in a sweeping cloak
        gathered us in.

Torquing, a fish leaps over a hook.
        Who is to say
lightning won't make us whole? Who is to say?

The plow.
The grim victory of a foot plunged through the ice.

2.

Heaven is smaller than the earth.
An iron teaches flatness, but
a building, too, teaches flatness.
          We are caught up by
a man in a sweeping cloak of grief.

3.

I sit down by the gravesite to think.
I refuse to talk to you, though
you pursue me, down on one knee.
        A whip lash, a curved tail,

torquing. A fish leaps over
a hook. What led us to believe
        that leaves would never fall?
The end is the beginning; is over.

Resolution

Finished with the latening sky, I
will return to earth. Language
is irrelevant there. Tissue of rock
   to shelter me from the mean,

I will carve only what I crave,
the curve of choices behind my back
retracted or contained. Last night
   I watched egrets layer in a tree

like blooms of pale rust. Yes,
I saw you, reckless sleepers:
first closeness, then wander;
   nearest, then nearer.

v

In the Wake of Avoidable Tragedy

What little remains is clear: it is over.

The first and the last having gone
and returned, come and returned,

we have learned to welcome those
who make the place feel welcoming.

A guitar in the corner hoards the light,
says: you, in a collapsing world,

your eyes such sharp, undarkened things.

Interview

What have you brought with you?
Rough praises, and a wind without a roof.

What is rough praise?
The earth there strips away thick skin.

What is thick skin?
My family is close. But I am distant.

What is rough praise?
Above the plains, I saw a red sun rise, and fell.

Desert

And I, I, am a disbeliever? A fool?
Listen—each new letter will spin and fall
Into the ones preceding, and the antidote
To suffering is pain. When I say suffering

I mean: the need for comforters, for
Jobs and practices that burn up all the time.
When I say time: the ticks that burrow
In our skin and leave us old and feckless.

I met a man who told me secrets, once,
Walking along in the dark. I am that man.

Isaac After the Mountain

Once there was another brother and he was
    My brother, tall and strong, he

Swung me through the long air, laughing,
    Both of us would laugh.

Why did he leave? Every afternoon
    I stand out in the fading light,

Watching for his camels.
    This, I hope, is prayer.

The Failed Prophet Addresses His Unborn Son

Build mansions from traipse, subtlety, candor,
the pith from behind these lived intentions—

let the walls sink into themselves year after year,
hiding gradually all the doors from sight

lest after-travelers should follow the firelight
inside and linger, softening your resolve. Here,

indifference plays the usher to approximation:
here resemblance is the best means of surrender.

This is your home—where time is always falling
over unmarked hills like laughter on the wind,

where washerwomen offer apples made of sand.
Without the flame, the candle has no calling.

Desert

Walking along in the dark, I am that man
You will not speak about, not here, where
Anyone could hear you—I am cold, blind
As lightning and its crackle; am defeatable

As winter grass and open as a razor.
But when the sky blew back—aftermath
Of a ragged dawn—you found my rage
Expendable. Therefore I traced

The outline of a dire plan. And since then,
What have I been doing? Nothing. Nothing.

Checklist for a Savior

Deliver us who have no spleen.
Belong to us, be length of days.
Turn us back to swans.

Cover us with bark of trees.
Miss your deadline to appear;
Make no apology. Appear.

Field Glass (Approach)

Stories, I have lost your strand. Lathe me
to invisible, frost me barren and estranged

as was foretold, but end this breakage
in sudden joy. In trees, the resin of hours

falls imperfectly; the vintage bartered from
the iris quarters, pale and incomplete. Why

must you swallow? In the book of this
migration, left-hand pages spill to null

unfinished, turning like fields in the weather.
Savage me with noise and scorn, letter me

with panic, but save these troubles;
lead me, in a new direction, home.

God of anchor and brace, God of hovering
and swoop, perennial God, mariner and bandit

of a God, God of white and wind, take pity.
Ladder and guide me; though all might pale,

I would wolverine on. Take me for talon, God,
that tears into the bony heart of God.

Notes

"Finishing the Hat" is by Stephen Sondheim, from *Sunday in the Park with George*.

Among the many poems in *The Wild Iris* I would love to have written is a "Matins" which Louise Glück begins, "Forgive me if I say I love you." "In the White Noise of the Evening" is a sometimes-negated, sometimes-homophonic translation, from English to English, of that poem.

"Lions Will Take You and I Will Not Care" is a reflection on the painting "A Lady Writing a Letter" (1665-6) by Jan Vermeer.

"Jacob and the Angels" responds to and reinterprets many verses in Genesis, but especially 25:26, 28:12, and 32:1.

The cohortative mood, related to the jussive and the imperative, expresses desire or (self-directed) command. "Cohortative with Pity" is for Lucie Brock-Broido, from whose words and phrases this poem has been arranged.

"Field Glass (Communion)" owes a debt to Denis Johnson's poem "The White Fires of Venus," from *The Incognito Lounge and Other Poems*, which includes these lines: "The remedy for loneliness / is in learning to admit / solitude as one admits / the bayonet: gracefully, / now that already / it pierces the heart."

Many of the words in each line of "Numerology" have been rearranged from the numbers that appear to the left of that line.

"Intimations of the Thaw" is mistranslated from a Japanese condolence card.

"Isaac After the Mountain" responds to and reinterprets Genesis 22:19 and 24:63.

Acknowledgments

Writing is not a solitary act. Many thanks to my family, friends, and colleagues, without whom, nothing. Extra special thanks to D.A. Powell, who helped me pick out an overcoat I can still wear these years later; to Stephanie Anderson, Adam Davis, Tom Hummel, Carey McHugh, Billy Merrell, Rob Ostrom, Cecily Parks, Andrew Seguin, and Lytton Smith, along with many others at Columbia, whose hands and ears and voices haunt and animate mine; and to Lucie Brock-Broido, Timothy Donnelly, Eamon Grennan, and Priscilla Becker for their enabling constraints. Thanks, as well, to Kim's Books and Music at Broadway and 113th, z"l, where many of these poems were written.

I am grateful to the following journals and their editors for publishing some of the poems in this manuscript:

EOAGH, The Greensboro Review, No Tell Motel, Pleiades, PresenTense, Redactions: Poetry and Poetics, RHINO, and *small.spiral.notebook.*

Benjamin Miller has studied at Harvard, Columbia, and the CUNY Graduate Center, and has taught writing at Columbia and Hunter College. His poems have appeared in *RHINO*, *Pleiades*, *The Greensboro Review*, and elsewhere; *Without Compass* is his first book. For more about Ben, visit majoringinmeta.net.